Old Glenisla,
Lintrathen and Airlie
John Alexander

The growing popularity of touring is evident in this picture of a mid 20th century motorist sitting beside his car and savouring the glen's scenic delights.

Acknowledgements

In my earlier life I did a few jobs in Blairgowrie. Glen Shee was the focus, as it was for some early and inglorious attempts to ski, so somehow my travels have tended to take me that way, with only occasional forays into Glen Isla. It has therefore been a delight of exploration to compile this little book both on the ground and by delving into various sources. These include numerous websites, some specifically subject related, others more general, notably: Friends of Dundee City Archives (for vehicle registration plates), Scotland's Places and Canmore of Historic Environment Scotland, Scottish Church Heritage Research – Places of Worship in Scotland and the treasure that is the map site of the National Library of Scotland.

Further Reading

The following were the principal books used by author during his research. None are available from Stenlake Publishing; please contact your local bookshop, reference library or search for them on the internet.

Baddeley, M. J. B., *Thorough Guides, Scotland* (Part 1), 1903.
Brander, Michael, *The Essential Guide to Highland Games*, 1992.
Brown, Rev. Thomas, *Annals of The Disruption*, 1884.
Gifford, John, *The Buildings of Scotland, Dundee and Angus*, 2012.
MacGibbon, David and Ross, Thomas, *The Castellated and Domestic Architecture of Scotland*, facsimile edition 1971.
Scottish Youth Hostels Association, *The Cairngorms, Deeside and Angus Glens: A Hosteller's Guide*, 1959.
Steven, Allistair, 'Britain's Highest Hillpath', article in *Scotland's Magazine*, Oct.1950.

© John Alexander, 2020
First published in the United Kingdom, 2020,
by Stenlake Publishing Ltd.
www.stenlake.co.uk
ISBN 978-1-84033-899-7

The publishers regret that they cannot supply copies of any pictures featured in this book.

Printed by
Blissetts, Unit E1-E8 Shield Drive,
West Cross Ind Pk, Brentford, TW8 9EX

Described in the 1880s as 'a plain modern mansion', when it was the property of Sir John George Smyth of Kinloch, Glenisla House occupies a narrow site on the east side of the glen south of Folda.

Introduction

Glen Isla is the most westerly of the glorious glens of Angus, with the River Isla emerging from Caenlochan Glen in the southern Grampians and flowing down a valley scoured and shaped by glacial erosion. At the northern end the glen is narrow and the hills steep, but lower down, the slopes become more gentle while the river, as a series of spectacular waterfalls, crashes through narrow gorges to reach the broad Strathmore.

The weather in these parts can be harsh and changeable, so life was never easy for the glen folk, but it was particularly tough in the middle years of the last millennium when cattle thieves, known as caterans periodically raided their land. They faced an even bigger onslaught in 1640 when, during a time of religious turmoil, the Earl of Argyll stripped the glen and burned the castles of the local laird, the Earl of Ogilvie. The raid generated such outrage that people still sing a song about it.

When the glen had recovered and time moved on, the upland areas became the preserve of sporting estates with lodges used in season by the owner's guests or rented by tenants. Small estates and farms ran sheep on the lower slopes or worked riverside fields for crops or livestock. Small local industries and mills provided some employment, with one mill also the background to a scandal. Small communities developed, clustered around either the church or that other essential in this challenging landscape, a bridge. Great houses were built, often as sporting lodges, but sometimes as retreats for wealthy incomers attracted by the peace and tranquility of the glen. As transport improved, people seeking the same attractions could arrive in their own vehicles or by striking out on foot from the nearest railway station or bus stop. Some visitors came and went in a day, while others opted for hostel or holiday accommodation and the trend has continued to evolve as local estates and enterprises have adapted to developments in modern tourism.

At the foot of the glen, the main road splits with one branch heading into the Perthshire town of Alyth, which has long been a focus for many of the glen's activities and services. The other road follows the line of the river and in particular its main tributary, the Melgam Water, which became a valuable source of water for Dundee centered on the Loch of Lintrathen. The place where the two rivers meet, to the south of Lintrathen, became the site for a great castle, and by extension the outrage of 1640, but as with the upper reaches of the glen Lintrathen, Airlie and surrounding areas have since settled into a more peaceable form of rural life.

Mansions like Craigisla House became a feature of the lower glen in the late Victorian period.

Modern road users, confined in their motor vehicles to a narrow strip of well-surfaced highway, don't see the ancient tracks through the hills that were familiar routes to their forebears who travelled on foot or horseback. Bands of marauders known as caterans, smugglers, and others actually engaged in lawful pursuits knew the path between Glenisla and the north where the next significant place of occupation was Braemar, on what became Royal Deeside when Queen Victoria acquired Balmoral Castle. Her popularization of the Highlands and its many attractions inspired others to follow, and for some that meant spending time at a shooting lodge from where they could venture forth in pursuit of the local wildlife. One such lodge was Tulchan at the junction of Glen Brighty and Glen Isla, close by that ancient track through the hills, which local people continued to use in defiance of the deer hunters' desire for exclusivity.

Shooting lodges like Tulchan often looked like the large villas fringing towns and cities, not so much suited to the landscape as imposed on it. So too was the concept of the 'deer forest' a vast tract of hill land with few, if any, trees. The only trees at Tulchan were in its immediate surroundings, which helped to screen the building and protect it from winter storms, which do tend to happen in these parts. Deer stalking is not well understood by modern society, but it requires great skill on the part of a gamekeeper to spot a suitable animal and work around it downwind using the lie of the land to keep out of sight, while all the time keeping an eye on the quarry. Doing this in the company of a shooting tenant, who may not share the keeper's skills, makes this doubly difficult, especially in the final approach to get within range. These days the shot is often taken with a camera or by the keeper as part of a cull to maintain balance in the countryside, another skill that goes largely unheralded until things go wrong.

About a mile and a half south of Tulchan Lodge, two farms, Linns and Dalhally nestled at the base of the hills on the eastern side of the glen. Flowing past them were the combined waters of the Glencally, Algeilly and Altvraigy Burns, which merged into one just above the farms, and then tumbled over a series of waterfalls known collectively as The Linns – with slight variations between Scots and Gaelic, 'linn' means a waterfall, or pool. The Linns Farm, evidently named after the waterfalls, sat on the north side of the burn and, slightly lower down, Dalhally was on the south side but both were east of the Isla and with the road on the west, getting across the river could be difficult. In dry weather, at this elevation – just over 1,000 feet above sea level – the Isla was not very daunting, although this rickety-looking footbridge allowed people to cross dry shod even when the river was running high. The later road bridge improved access.

A number of farms and cottages were strung out along the valley to the south of Linns and Dalhally, with a couple situated to the east of the river although most were adjacent to the road on the west bank. Some of these buildings can be seen in the background of this view looking north past Presnerb Farm in the right foreground. Mainly a livestock farm, it was evidently still working as such when this picture was taken. The main farmhouse, rubble-built, harled and painted, is typical of such dwellings dating from the 19th or possibly late 18th century. Initially a tenanted property belonging to the Earl of Airlie it was later sold off as part of the smaller Achavan Estate, the name taken from another upland farm close to the Linns Bridge. As a sporting estate it ran to nearly 2,300 acres and included the 2,647 feet summit of the mountain Monameanach, so not exactly small. It has since adapted to the modern era with Presnerb as a holiday let.

Little Forter sits at an important junction where the road to and from the north of the glen splits, with one branch heading west to join the main road on the west side of the glen and another branch crossing the river to the east side. Dating from the late 18th or early 19th century, the fine single arched rubble stone bridge that forms the river crossing is seen in the foreground of this picture. Little Forter itself was described by the surveyors preparing Ordnance Survey maps in the mid 19th century as a farm and dwelling house 'with offices and lands attached, the property of the Earl of Airlie'. These surveyors went to a lot of trouble to ascertain the correct form and spelling of place names, asking local people for advice. They seemed to struggle a bit with Forter, with some folk saying Forter, and others Folda. Both names have become established with Folda applied to the village on the east side of the glen.

Flanked by the hills to the north and the imposing Mount Blair to the south, a *bealach*, a hill pass cuts through to link Glen Shee in the west with Glen Isla. Tumbling down the pass, the Balloch Burn merges with the Isla at Forter, a meeting point of glen and pass that made this a point of strategic importance in the turbulent 16th century. It was like a back door to the Airlie lands and so, to bolster its defence, James, 5th Lord Ogilvie of Airlie built Forter Castle about 1560. Typical of the period it consisted of a main tower with a smaller entrance tower containing a stair to the first floor, which continued to the upper floors in a turret built into the angle formed by the two towers. This arrangement of offset towers made for stronger defence, but it failed, because in 1640 the Earl of Argyll raided the glen, drove off the cattle and burned the castle. It remained in a ruinous state until its restoration in the 1990s

The road between Glenisla and Glenshee was given the number B951 when roads were classified in the 1920s. It has always been an important link, which this smartly dressed couple discovered when they stopped for a picnic on the narrow strip of ground between the road and the Shee Water/Black Water. Traffic was lighter in those days and the two seem unconcerned that the rear wheel of their motorcycle has been left protruding into the road, which winds away behind them to the bridge at Cray and on to Glenisla. Cray House is in the woods on the other side of the river. The couple's vehicle, an A .J. S. motorcycle and sidecar, was registered in Dundee in 1920, which helps to date both this picture and the one on the facing page. Built at Wolverhampton, the A. J. S. was popular at the time having established a number of world records, but with mounting financial difficulties the company went out of business in 1931.

The two people shown on the facing page with their motorcycle also appear in this photograph, taken either before or after they stopped for their roadside picnic – sadly it is not known what direction they were travelling in and therefore the order in which the pictures were taken, but they are splendid. They offer a real insight into the social history of people emerging from the shadows of the First World War and discovering the delights of the countryside within easy reach of the city, so long as they had the means to do it. The pictures could have been taken as a record of the couple's first outing with their new pride and joy, or perhaps for publicity purposes, although neither possibility solves a central puzzle; who took the photographs? This one shows the couple on the B951 at its junction with the road to the head of the glen, which is seen going into the distance past the ruined Forter Castle and Meikle Forter Farm. The motorcycle is pointing south to Altaltan and Brewlands Bridge.

Just south of Little Forter on the west side of the glen is Altaltan Cottage, seen here in 1906 with the distinctive Mount Blair behind. The hill (or mountain) features in one of the highlights of the glen's social scene, the Highland Games, held at the Games Haugh, a natural amphitheatre beside the river almost adjacent to Altaltan. Organized by the Glenisla Highland and Friendly Society, the event is held annually in late August. The programme includes all the usual competitions for piping, Highland dancing, children's races and throwing events for those big men in big kilts culminating in the activity that gives a Highland Games its special appeal, tossing the caber. When gamekeeping and stalking were more common in the glen, the games also held a rifle shooting event, but the Glenisla Games still has a specialty all of its own, a hill race up Mount Blair, all 2,441 feet of it.

Fixed bridges were not always where people who lived in isolated cottages needed them and at Altaltan people used the clever piece of engineering shown in this picture to get across the river. It looks like a chair with wheels on the sides, which ran along cables and was propelled by the occupants pulling it along by the upper cables. A further rope attached to the chair allowed its users to haul it, when needed, to the side of the river they were on. One service the users of the chair bridge might have wanted to get to was the post office at Folda on the east side of the glen, which is seen here in a picture taken either before or during the First World War.

Post offices in rural locations often shared premises with something else, like a shop, which accounts for this picture of Folda Post Office looking somewhat different to the one shown on the previous page. This earlier building doubled as a school, set up by the Society in Scotland for Propagating Christian Knowledge, a charitable body formed in Edinburgh by Royal Charter, in 1709. With strong links to the Established Church of Scotland its schools were usually placed in areas where it was felt desirable to combat Catholic, Episcopalian and, by extension, Jacobite influence, or where the provision of a parish school was absent or inadequate. These schools charged no fees and with a strong emphasis on the three R's were often popular with poorer people. Teaching was in English although teachers had to be bi-lingual in both it and Gaelic and later in the 18th century the Society sought to develop an inclusive bilingual programme. The Society's schools made a difference in remote communities, but were consigned to history when the Education Act of 1872 came into force.

The evolution of the post office at Folda is completed by this picture, which was actually used as a postcard in 1969, although the picture may predate that. The earlier signs advertising services like a public telephone and telegraph office have been replaced by a red telephone box, once a familiar sight on street corners and in rural spots where they provided a lifeline for local people and stranded tourists. The post offices in the glen could postmark letters with their own hand-stamp, but when these went through the sorting office in Alyth they were stamped again (like the inset above from the postcard on the facing page), and incoming mail had to be addressed as 'by Alyth'. Folda is the most northerly element of an extended village made up of a number of houses and other buildings strung out along the east side of the glen. To the south of Folda, the large Glenisla House is situated at a location called Inverharity, a name with clear Gaelic origins, 'inbhir' meaning the mouth of a burn or river as in Inverness.

The Gaelic influence continues a little further south with this row of cottages known as Balnamenoch, seen here in a picture from 1906. The first part of the name is a shortening of 'baile' meaning a village or town. The second part could mean middle, as in middle field or land and could thus be the same as Ballymena in Northern Ireland. That may or may not be right, but what it does indicate is that although Angus Council portrays its area as the heartland of the Picts, in the glens, at least, the Gaels were very much in evidence. The Picts, who inhabited eastern Scotland north from the Forth estuary to Orkney, left no written record, but did pass on some identifiable place names and archaeological remains in the form of wonderful carved stones and jewelry. Their language, gleaned mainly from place names, shows similarities to the ancestor of Welsh. The Balnamenoch houses, like most others by the roadside south of Folda, sat on higher ground facing the river. Between road and river is an area of flattish land, which accounts for the farm cart on the left of the picture.

A photographer was evidently busy in the glen in 1906, because this picture was also taken in that year. It shows Alrick, a large livestock farm and steading about a mile to the south of Balnamenoch, but on the west side of the river. Built on the lower slopes of Mount Blair as they flatten off toward the river and the Alrick Burn to the south, this location appears to have been occupied for thousands of years, because a settlement site, field system and cairn from the late Bronze Age were discovered a few hundred yards to the west of the house in the 1970s. The settlement was made up of a group of circular houses, a couple of which appeared similar to a type found nearby at Dalrulzion in Perthshire, which suggests a related local population. The site also revealed evidence of occupation and land working from the period before agricultural improvement in the 18th century, indicating perhaps that farming has continued at Alrick for over 3,000 years.

A minor road snakes eastward through the hills from the evocatively named Blacklunans in Glen Shee and then follows the line of the Alrick Burn down into Glen Isla at Brewlands. A traveller on the road could then head north or south on either side of the glen by crossing the elegant single-arched Brewlands Bridge. Constructed using rubble masonry the bridge was built in the first half of the 19th century, thanks in large measure to Thomas Rattray, proprietor of nearby Brewlands House. It is seen here looking north from a position sufficiently close to the water on the river's west bank for the photographer to have got wet feet. A road junction with a river crossing in hill country was always going to be a magnet for people and a little village, or more accurately a hamlet grew up; its name Brewlands Bridge, a measure of the importance of the bridge to the local area. Although superseded in 1970 by a modern replacement the old bridge remains in situ.

The hamlet of Brewlands Bridge never amounted to more than a few houses, most of which are shown in this picture looking north along the road that ran up the west side of the glen. The houses on the right backed onto the river, and if the photographer had swung round to the right he or she would have been looking across the bridge. The low building on the right was a smithy, ideally situated for farmers and gentry from miles around to come to have their horses shod and cart and carriage wheels repaired. Three pedestrians sauntering toward the camera suggest that, at the time the picture was being taken, the road wasn't busy. It does a little shimmy as it passes to the left of the building that faces camera, known as the 'Schoolhouse'. It was neither a parish nor society school, but is marked as an 'industrial school' on mid 19th century maps, the kind of institution where children from disadvantaged backgrounds could be educated, often in craft skills.

Backed by the hills and seemingly cradled by trees, Brewlands House is the 'big house' at the centre of the estate. Situated to the south of Brewlands Bridge on the west bank of the river it is seen here in a picture from the mid 20th century. For some time it was the home of the Rattray family, represented in the early 19th century by Thomas Rattray. He carried out major improvements to the estate and area, such as construction of the bridge over the Isla, and he also played a leading role in local affairs, as the story on the following pages will show. He was a man of his time and since then the estate owners have also sought to tune their activities to prevailing times. Many estate cottages have been turned into holiday lets, farming continues as do the traditional activities of a sporting estate, but the wildlife, including delightful red squirrels, is more usually often shot with a camera and pigeons are of the clay variety.

To the south of Brewlands was another large house, Auchenleish, and although separated by a third of a mile the two were near enough for such dwellings to be regarded as next door neighbours. Built in the early 20th century, Auchenleish is seen here in a picture from the 1930s, at a time when the house was occupied by Lady Henrietta Fraser, widow of Sir Andrew Henderson Leith Fraser who had a distinguished career in the Indian Colonial Service, latterly as Lieutenant Governor of Bengal. Lady Fraser herself had strong connections to the country as the daughter of a Colonel in the Indian army. She spoke Hindustani and was able to assist her husband in matters affecting women, and in particular aristocratic women in purdah. At the end of their colonial careers, people often retired to large houses like Auchenleish, which provided a financial boost to the local economy. Lady Fraser's association with the house is remembered in the name of a nearby field.

A guidebook, published in 1902, exhorted its readers to head north on foot up the road on the west side of the glen and strike over the shoulder of the hill, Druim Dearg, to cross the river by a bridge close to the inn. This 'inn' was Glenisla Hotel, described in the book as 'a comfortable little house' with a garden containing some interesting ferns, and the walker was urged not to miss it, because as the book inferred this was the only hotel in the glen. Sadly the guidebook's author made no comment on the nearby bridge, which was an early example of a suspension bridge designed and built by John Justice (Junior) of Justice & Company of Dundee in 1824. Such bridges are familiar in the modern world, but at the time the technology was in its infancy. Set above the water on stone abutments it was about 60 feet across and although looking somewhat spindly must have been a huge boon to the community, especially for children positioned, as it was, directly opposite the parish school.

The name Kirkton of Glenisla refers not to the glen, but to Glenisla Parish because this is where its kirk and school were situated. In the days when folk made a determined effort to go to the kirk it was for some a very big commitment because the parish was about sixteen miles long and nearly six miles wide, so some people had a long walk to worship. The site at the west end of the village had been occupied by an earlier church dedicated to the Blessed Virgin until 1821 when a new building designed by the architect David Whyte was erected. It was a simple oblong rubble masonry structure with a bellcote, and had a large seating capacity for a sparsely populated parish. The interior was refitted in 1952, but as the Church of Scotland continued to contract, the building was taken over by local people who formed a charity to keep it going.

Following the Disruption of 1843, when about 40% of ministers and a larger proportion of parishioners left the established Church of Scotland to form the Free Church, Kirkton acquired another church, but not immediately. When the initial schism occurred only a handful of local people showed any inclination to break away and faced mockery from others in the glen. They travelled to Cray in Glenshee to worship and arranged for visiting ministers to preach in a makeshift tent, but struggled to attract more than a handful of people. Then a vacancy occurred in the Parish Church and remarkably a minister was imposed on the congregation against their will – exactly the situation that had led to the Disruption taking place.

As if a dam had burst the outraged parishioners met in the school and voted to join the Free Church. Meetings with visiting preachers continued in John Crombie's cart shed and in the open while funds were raised, but importantly two of the leading landowners, Mr Rattray of Brewlands and Mr Spalding of Broomhall supported the congregation. Mr Rattray gave land in the village for the new church seen on the facing page, the imposing manse seen here and a school. The church, with some 300 sittings, was erected just to the north of the Parish Church and completed in 1849 before winter set in. The following year a new minister was appointed and Glenisla, the parish that came out in support of the Free Church five years after the initial walk-out, became a big story in one of the country's most significant social upheavals.

Kirkton of Glenisla is sometimes described as a hamlet, which is not quite accurate because a hamlet generally refers to a village without a church, and Kirkton had two churches, two manses and two church schools, so not a hamlet then, just a very small village. It also extended eastwards to Woodend, the small group of cottages seen here. The cottage closest to camera, at the end of the row on the left, was the local post office, which according to the sign was also equipped with a public telephone. Tucked in beyond the row of cottages is a knoll where the parish war memorial, a simple cairn, was erected to honour the fallen of the First World War. Roselea Cottage, the single building in the distance, was later used by Angus Council to house a roadman. The sole vehicle on the road here, parked well out from the side, may have been the car used by the photographer and left in a prominent position to 'dress' the picture – photographers did that sort of thing.

The glen, and particularly the area to the east and south of Kirkton, will have been buzzing with gossip because of events that took place at East Mill in 1765. In January of that year Thomas Ogilvie, whose home it was, married Katherine Nairn. He was 40 years old, she half his age. Things went wrong when Thomas' younger brother Patrick, a Lieutenant in the army, returned home and began a very public affair with Katherine. Within a short time Thomas was dead, arsenic poisoning being suspected. Katherine and Patrick were arrested, tried and found guilty. Patrick, protesting his innocence, was hanged but Katherine was pregnant and could not be executed until she gave birth. And she didn't hang because she escaped from prison. But were either she or Patrick guilty and was the evidence, given by a female cousin possibly in league with another of Thomas' brothers Alexander who inherited the property, reliable? The verdict could have been unsafe, potentially a tragic miscarriage of justice.

Bare trees and newly-born lambs are clear indicators that it was springtime when this picture was taken in 1909 at the Freuchies, the collective name for the farms, East and West Freuchie. The name, which was derived from the Gaelic 'fraoch', means heather, or heathery. The natural cycle of a ewe means that she will carry a lamb through the winter months and be ready to give birth in the spring, which is why lambs are always associated with the season and Easter. It's an intense and crucial part of the sheep farmer's year and although many ewes give birth unaided, the farmer will want to be on hand night and day in case of problems. As soon as they are born, lambs are bonded with their mothers and when feeding is progressing well they are put in a field to allow the ewes to graze the fresh grass, supplemented if necessary and thus make milk for the hungry lambs. That appears to be the stage this flock is at, in a scene that will have been replicated at hill farms up and down the glen.

After flowing roughly west-east for about a mile as it passes Kirkton, the river turns south again, give or take a few meandering changes of direction. The main road runs along the east bank while strung out along the west bank, a number of farms and houses, including Easter and Wester Peathaugh, Cammock and Whitehills were effectively sandwiched between the river and steeply rising high ground to the west. This was clearly fertile ground and a good place to live because evidence of a Bronze Age settlement site with a field system was discovered at Easter Cammock in the 1980s. A limekiln dating from about 1800 has also been recorded at Whitehills. So this was good farming land on the west side of the river, but with the inconvenience for people of having to go a long way round to cross the water unless they took the potentially risky option of using one of a couple of fords. That changed in the early 20th century when the ford at Whitehills was replaced by bridge. It is seen here looking south with the distinctive Knockshannoch Lodge in the background.

The popular theory regarding round buildings is they had no corners for the devil to hide in. That is certainly the story told about churches and it also has been said of Knockshannoch House. The Celtic/Gaelic word 'cnoc' means 'a small round hill', so maybe the building's shape was intended to echo that; it is certainly idiosyncratic, although the dormer windows on the upper floor offered many devil-hiding corners. Erected in 1888 as a shooting lodge about a mile and half east of Kirkton of Glenisla it's not just the house, but the kitchen wing and a number of outbuildings that were circular in plan. After the Second World War the house became one of the growing number of Scottish Youth Hostels Association (SYHA) premises that were being opened up for adventurous young people who were taking to the country on foot or by bicycle to explore wild landscapes at modest cost.

Scotland for Ski-ing

* LEARN TO SKI AT THE S.Y.H.A.

SKI COURSE AT GLENISLA HOSTEL, PERTHSHIRE

For £6 10s a week you get
* ALL MEALS AND BEDNIGHTS
* TUITION BY EXPERT INSTRUCTORS
* TRANSPORT TO SNOW SLOPES

Skis on Hire.   Experienced skiers can also join the courses.

FROM JANUARY 31 till APRIL 11

Write to Gen. Secy., S.Y.H.A., 7 Bruntsfield Cres., Edinburgh, 10.

The shape of Knockshannoch lent itself to use as a hostel with a large circular hall and circular gallery leading to the upstairs dormitories. As a hostel it had 80 beds and all the usual facilities of kitchen, dining room, games and quiet rooms, and for wet days the warden could offer card games, dominoes, draughts and two table tennis tables – life's pleasures were simpler then! And the hostel had one other main attraction, in the days before Scottish ski resorts were fully developed, Glen Isla and particularly neighbouring Glen Shee, were regarded as good places for skiing and the SYHA used the hostel as a skiing centre. Courses were held and hostellers with more experience could hire skis by the day or week. In post hostelling days Knockshannoch became an adventure centre, so it could be argued that it consistently fulfilled its purpose as a place for people to stay while engaging in country pursuits, it's just that the pursuits have changed with the changing times.

An earlier Glenmarkie Lodge existed in this isolated moorland location before 1900/1901 when, the building seen in this picture from 1906 was erected to the designs of Dundee architects Mills and Shepherd. As well as the main house, they designed other estate buildings including stables and kennels – everything a well-appointed hunting/shooting lodge would need. The client was Arthur James Cox, a member of the Cox family who owned and operated the huge Camperdown Jute Works. One of the largest factories of its kind in Dundee, it covered a site of 30 acres dominated by one of the city's industrial landmarks, an ornate chimney nearly 300 feet high known as Cox's Stack. The family donated a park, baths and library to the local community, but the industry was notable for the contrast between financial privations endured by mill workers and the owners' wealth, a disparity that the building of a large sporting lodge in a remote glen tended to underline.

Sitting at the base of Cuilt Hill, Glenhead Farm lived up to its name by also being at the head of a sparsely populated glen. Flowing down it was the Back Water fed by water from Glentaitney, Glendamff, the Hole Burn and numerous smaller streams. In the 1870s the river attracted the attention of engineers seeking a clean water supply for Dundee by expanding the Loch of Lintrathen. Ninety years later, the city's engineers were back, this time to create a new holding reservoir by erecting an embankment dam, 140 feet high and 1,800 feet long, between the Hill of Bellaty and Creigh Hill. Work began in March 1964, but instead of excavating down to bedrock at depths of up to 160 feet they chose to create a foundation for the dam by grouting and consolidating the alluvial deposits. Holding 5,000,000 gallons, the completed Backwater Reservoir was inaugurated by the Queen in 1969. A perimeter road gives access to Glenhead Farm, which no longer looks down the glen, but across a shimmering sheet of water.

To the south of Knockshannoch the main glen road leaves the riverside at Needs and runs east of Craiglea Hill to Dykends where it divides, heading south to Bridge of Craigisla and east to Lintrathen. The fork in the road is seen to the left of the scar on the hill in the centre of the picture. That scar was a gravel pit, or quarry; workers' houses can be seen alongside. The whole of Glen Isla from Forter to Needs is flanked by terraces of sand, gravel and football-sized boulders laid down at the edges of the glacier that scoured the shape of the glen. The glacial melt water appears to have pushed into the valley later occupied by the road, and deposited the sand and gravel extracted by the quarry. In the foreground is the bridge over the Back Water, which changes name to Melgam Water just beyond this point. The foreground cottage was a smithy, a useful facility in an industrial setting.

Ballintore Castle, situated to the north of Bridgend of Lintrathen, was not really a castle, but a large Victorian mansion. It was built in 1859/60 for David Lyon, a member of the Lyon family of Glenogil, a former MP who made his money though plantations in the West Indies and compensation awarded when slavery was abolished. For Ballintore he engaged the architect William Burn, a leading exponent of the Scots Baronial style of architecture much favoured for such grand, perhaps grandiose houses. Designed to impress, the multi-faceted roofs, turrets and towers were ill-suited to Scottish weather, which took its toll of a building that will have been difficult and costly to maintain. Lyon died in 1872 and over time, with occupancy latterly limited to use as a seasonal shooting lodge the structure succumbed to the ravages of dry rot and was abandoned in the 1960s. A 'listed' structure, it was placed on the Buildings at Risk register in 1994 and compulsorily purchased by Angus Council with a view to finding a restoring owner.

Situated due south of Dykends between Craiglea Hill and the distinctive Knock of Formal, Fornethy House was completed in 1915. The architects, Fryers and Penman were both trained at Glasgow School of Art and set up practice in the city, eventually moving to Largs. They developed a working relationship with the wealthy Coats family of Paisley who owned the largest thread producing business in the world and it was for them that they started work on Fornethy in 1912. It wasn't titled a 'lodge' as so many large houses in the glen were, but a house, a summer residence for a prominent west coast family. They must have loved it, the glorious setting away from the wet west, but by the 1950s the thread business was facing stiff competition, the family had moved on and the house became a residential school for children from Glasgow. Some youngsters enjoyed the change from city surroundings, but others disliked it, comparing the strict regime to their idea of life in a prisoner of war camp. Either way it closed in the 1990s.

A sizeable, if scattered, community developed around Bridge of Craigisla and alongside the river and Kilry Burn, but there was no convenient place for the people to worship until 1876 when the Kilry Church was built. Situated between Glenisla and Lintrathen Parishes it served a subsidiary parish formed out of elements detached from the two older ones. The new entity was known as a Quoad Sacra parish, which meant it could provide religious, but not the civil functions of a full parish church. Occupying a corner site at the Dykehead road junction, it was a small church with a large manse alongside. Constructed using harled rubble walls and a dressed stone bellcote, the building has since been modified with a new entrance and porch, and a fine war memorial stained glass window. It has also proved to be a survivor as one of the churches that merged to form the Isla Parishes in 2005. Prior to the building of the church, a school had been established in the locality by the Society for Propagating Christian Knowledge, but unlike the church it has been superseded by the Isla Primary School, situated just over a mile to the east at Easter Peel Farm.

At a bend in the river, just upstream of the Bridge of Craigisla, water was diverted to drive the Mill of Craigisla, or Milnacraig, seen here to the right of the bridge. In the 18th and earlier centuries mills were integral to the running of estates through a system known as thirlage, which tied tenants to a mill. During the 19th century many tenants bought out their obligations, others were simply freed and the system died out. Millers took over and fewer, larger mills, run on more commercial lines, became dominant, with many small mills falling into disuse. To the south of the bridge lie a number of properties with 'Craig' in their name, one of which, described in the mid 19th century as a 'small but handsome mansion', was known as Cotton of Craig. This had nothing to do with cloth and instead referred to a cot town, a place occupied by cottars or tied farm workers. Such folk were unlikely to live in a mansion however small, so the name probably came from the time before the agricultural improvements that also changed the way mills were run. The house was later enlarged as the grand Craigisla House.

The bridge and mill are seen here in a view that looks to the north and west, with a backdrop of the hills that form the county boundary with Perthshire, but which have since largely been obscured by tree growth. Downstream from the bridge, the river also heads for Perthshire, but before that it enters a deep rocky ravine and drops about 60 feet through a series of cascades that make up one of the country's most spectacular waterfalls. A path leads to it from a small car park on the site from where this picture was taken. Doubly awesome when the river is running high and the falls meld into one, the waterfall is known as the Reekie Linn, a name that clearly refers to the fine mist of spray thrown up by the crashing water – the old Scots word 'reek' means smoke or vapour. It's a modest name for such magnificence, but another mile or so downstream is another waterfall with a really memorable name, the Slug of Auchrannie. It's also a slightly odd name given that the river here is anything but sluggish and races through the gorge with sufficient force to have interested engineers keen to harness it for hydro-electric power.

Dundee Town Council took over the company that supplied water to the town in 1869 and appointed commissioners to oversee provision. Seeking improved supplies they appointed one of the foremost water engineers in the country John Frederic Bateman. He examined two schemes, one to draw water from the Isla, the other, put forward by the old water company's engineer John Leslie, to utilise the Loch of Lintrathen as a reservoir. Bateman preferred the latter scheme, but the Dundee Water Commissioners demurred in favour of a pipeline that Bateman thought impractical. He was right, it failed and consequently the small Loch of Lintrathen was enlarged as a reservoir in 1875. Impounded by an embankment beside Bridgend of Lintrathen the water flows over this impressive weir into the Melgum Water and onward to Dundee.

The Lintrathen Reservoir Main Lodge was erected to the west of the main village. Originally planned by John Leslie, it was designed about 1890 by his successor at the Dundee Water Commission, civil engineer, James Watson who also instigated the landscaping around the loch and planting – he evidently liked the look of monkey puzzle trees. The loch, or reservoir as it was when this picture was taken, can be seen in the background. Designed in the Scots Baronial style with its turret, crenellated tower and crow stepped gables the lodge is mainly built of red sandstone, but edged with dressed yellow stone. The entrance to the drive was finished off with ornate cast iron gates. Described in the 1930s as a 'very handsome lodge' in 'tasteful surroundings' and 'in fine keeping with the loch and grand scenery around it', it has since been given a B listing.

Bridgend of Lintrathen is seen in this picture from 1909. Written on the back is a note stating that it is 'a view of the village beside the loch', and that 'our little grocer's shop is at the bottom of the card, Shoppie Geordie we call him, he keeps every thing you could mention in that little shop'. 'Shoppie Geordie' was George Smith, who ran the little Lintrathen Store, which can also be seen, as it was about 1930, on the front cover. That picture amply demonstrates the wide range of merchandise that George Smith stocked and that he did indeed 'keep every thing you could mention'. Outside on display are tins of biscuits and an array of advertisements for laundry services, tobacco, tea and oil. The later shop was situated on the site of a former smithy, a rural institution that often gave way to the motor industry when actual horse power was replaced by that generated by the internal combustion engine. George Smith also sold petrol. The building has since continued to be used for commercial activities.

In the years following the First World War communities large and small raised funds to erect memorials to those who had lost their lives in the conflict. In towns and cities this resulted in impressive displays of generosity and some imposing monuments, but in less populous rural areas smaller, simpler memorials were erected that often conveyed something more personal and poignant. Everyone will have known the men whose names were inscribed. The memorial erected to the fallen of Lintrathen Parish was unveiled on 13th June 1921 by Mrs Spence, wife of Dundee's Lord Provost Spence who ceremonially unwrapped Union flags to reveal a simple Aberdeen granite column, surmounted by a cross and surrounded by a neat enclosure. Eleven names were listed and to these were added two more after the Second World War.

'Geordie' Smith published a series of local postcards, one of which was this picture showing Cairnhall, a farm close to the River Isla, west of Bridgend. The card was sent to an address in Fife with the message; 'This is the farm where I am spending my holiday and having grand fun'. The collection of buildings looks grand too (and there were other buildings behind the photographer). The farmhouse, with a large wooden cask propped up to collect and dispense rainwater, is on the left. Beyond it is a wooden shed and to the right an outhouse clad in corrugated iron, a material that became a feature of rural Scotland from the late 19th century. The iron sheets were nailed onto a wooden frame and painted, and with interiors often lined with boards this type of building was used for churches, shops, houses and sheds. Fitted with a proper door, it's tempting to think that this one at Cairnhall may not have been a simple shed, but perhaps temporary accommodation where the holidaymaker who sent the card was staying.

Flowing out of the reservoir and tumbling over the attractive Lintrathen Falls, the Meglam Water effectively splits Bridgend in two with the Lintrathen Parish Church and manse situated on the north bank, while the main body of the village is to the south. The manse, seen here in a picture from 1909, appears to have been built in two phases, with the original, early 19th century, house on the right and a mid century extension facing camera on the left. The church is more ancient, with one having existed on the site as St. Medan's Church since the 13th century or earlier. A new church, built in 1802, was extended with the addition of a north aisle in 1875. With church attendance falling, the building was closed in 2011 and sold. The manse has also become a private dwelling renamed as Melgam House.

Airlie Castle was built in the mid 15th century on the promontory formed by the converging Melgam Water and River Isla. The steep river valleys made it a strong defensible position, approachable only from the east across ground cut with a ditch, which may have been spanned by a drawbridge for added security. A high wall surrounded a courtyard with an entrance guarded by a tall tower that incorporated a range of defensive features that included the door itself, a portcullis and a flue for dropping missiles on attackers. It was strong, but not strong enough because in 1640 James Ogilvie, the 1st Earl of Airlie, marched his men off to support King Charles 1 in the religious wars that followed the signing of the National Covenant in 1638. Taking advantage of his absence, Archibald Campbell, Earl of Argyll, Ogilvie's powerful enemy, marched into the glen with 5,000 of his clansmen, intent on wreaking havoc.

The Earl had left his eldest son James, Lord Ogilvie, in charge, but with only a few men he was unable to resist the force deployed by Argyll who destroyed Forter Castle higher up the glen, and demanded the surrender of Airlie Castle. What followed has been immortalised in a ballad, *Bonnie House of Airlie* that describes the token resistance of the Countess of Airlie before Argyll and his men ransacked and burned the castle leaving it a smouldering ruin. Although not untypical in the brutal world of inter-clan feuding, different versions of the song have elevated the event from wanton destruction and brutality, to an act of treachery and outrage, compounded by atrocity. The ravaging of the glen – 'they have not left him in all his lands a cock to crow day' – was undoubtedly dreadful for the Ogilvie family who were forced to abandon their ruined buildings and move to Cortachy Castle at the foot of Glen Clova.

Despite all that had happened to him and his family, the Earl's support for Charles I remained undimmed and he and his sons joined the Royalist campaign against the Covenanters led by the Marquis of Montrose. In 1645 Thomas, his second son, was killed at the Battle of Inverlochy and James, Lord Ogilvie, was captured at the Battle of Philiphaugh, but smuggled out of prison by his sister. The Earl himself led the charge at the Battle of Kilsyth, which routed the Covenanters. He was eventually pardoned for his 'rebellion' and returned to his lands and titles, but the family's continued support for the Stewart cause came close to them losing the lot (again) after the Jacobite uprising in 1745/46. They survived, Airlie Castle remained their property and, in the late 18th century, the new mansion seen on the left of this picture was built inside the old curtain wall. In 1900 the 11th Earl of Airlie, fighting for the British Army, was killed leading his regiment at the Battle of Diamond Hill in the South African War. He was honoured at the junction of Glens Prosen and Clova with a memorial that replicated the tower of Airlie Castle.